# Addison Wesley
# Science & Technology 3

W9-AYF-774

## Matter and Materials
•
# Magnetism

Nora L. Alexander
Grade 3 Program Authors:

Nora L. Alexander     Carole Moult

Doug Herridge     Ricki Wortzman

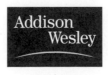

Addison
Wesley

Toronto

**Coordinating & Developmental Editors**
Jenny Armstrong
Lynne Gulliver

| **Editor** | **Researchers** |
| Jackie Dulson | Louise MacKenzie |
| | Rosanne Green, Colborne Communications Centre |

**Reviewers**
Lesley Corry, Robert Bateman Public School, Ottawa-Carleton District School
Board
Jane Stone, Valley View Public School, Durham District School Board

Pearson Education Canada would like to thank the teachers and consultants
who reviewed and field-tested this material.

**Design**
Pronk&Associates

Copyright © 2000 Pearson Education Canada Inc., Toronto, Ontario

All rights reserved. This publication is protected by copyright, and permission
should be obtained from the publisher prior to any prohibited reproduction,
storage in a retrieval system, or transmission in any form or by any means,
electronic, mechanical, photocopying, recording, or likewise. For information
regarding permission, write to the Permissions Department.

The information and activities presented in this book have been carefully
edited and reviewed. However, the publisher shall not be liable for any
damages resulting, in whole or part, from the reader's use of this material.

Brand names that appear in photographs of products in this textbook are
intended to provide students with a sense of the real-world applications of
science and technology and are in no way intended to endorse specific
products.

ISBN 0–201–64977–2

This book contains recycled product and is acid free.
Printed and bound in Canada.

2  3  4  5 – TCP – 04 03 02 01 00

# Magnetism

**W**elcome to the world of magnetism and charged materials. A look at charged materials and magnets a long, long time ago led to discoveries in electricity. Magnetism makes electricity. Because electricity is so important, learning about magnetism and charged materials is also important.

## Now you will find out:

- what materials are magnetic
- how to make a static electric charge
- where magnets and charged materials are found
- how you can use magnets to move a boat or sled that you build

Launch: Marguerite's
Magnetic Tour . . . . . . . . . . . . . . 2

1: About Magnets . . . . . . . . . . . . . 4

2: What Does a Magnet
Pick Up?. . . . . . . . . . . . . . . . . . 6

3: Does the Metal Matter? . . . . . . . 8

4: Measuring Magnetic
Strength . . . . . . . . . . . . . . . . . . 10

5: What Makes It Magnetic? . . . . . 12

6: Does Magnetism Pass
Through Materials? . . . . . . . . . . 14

7: Will Magnetism Pass
Through Water?. . . . . . . . . . . . . 16

8: Making Magnets . . . . . . . . . . . 18

9: The Poles of a Magnet . . . . . . . 20

10: Finding the North Pole . . . . . . 22

11: Charged Materials. . . . . . . . . 24

12: Static Electricity in Your Life . . . 26

13: Lightning: Nature's
Static Electricity. . . . . . . . . . . 28

14: How Important Is Distance? . . . 30

Design Project: Magnetic
Boats and Sleds. . . . . . . . . . . . 32

Unit Review . . . . . . . . . . . . . . . 38

Glossary. . . . . . . . . . . . . . . . . . 43

# Marguerite's Magnetic Tour

## Get Started

Meet Marguerite. She will take you on a tour through her home to find where magnets are used. You will be surprised how many things use a magnet in some way.

> A MAGNET HOLDS MY EARRINGS ON. ANOTHER HOLDS MY BACKPACK CLOSED!

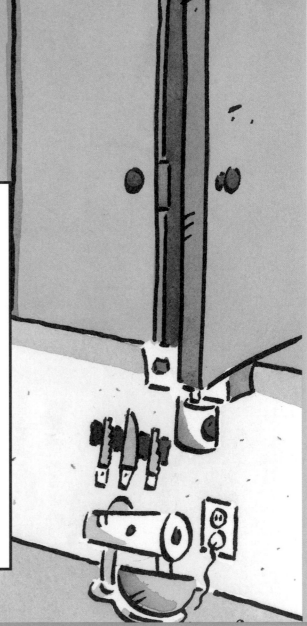

## Marguerite's Magnet-Hunting Hints

- The kitchen curtains stay in place on the steel door with magnets.

- The cupboard doors stay shut because of magnets.

- The paper clip holder uses a magnet.

- Information is put on computer disks, video cassettes, compact discs, and cassette tapes as tiny pieces of magnets.

### Work On It

1. Make a list of the things that use magnets in Marguerite's house. Marguerite's magnet-hunting tips will help you get started.

2. Go on a magnet search in your home.

3. Circle the things on the list that you also have in your home.

4. What other magnets can you find in your home? Add them to your list.

### Communicate

1. Draw a picture of the magnetic strip inside the door of a refrigerator.

2. Explain why the magnet is there.

# 1 About Magnets

Magnets have been around for a very long time. The ancient Greeks found that a special type of rock was a magnet. These rocks were often found in an area of Greece called Magnesia. Perhaps that is where the name magnet came from.

The rock that was found in Greece is called magnetite. It is a magnet found in nature. Magnetite can be found all over the world.

Today, magnets are very important. Magnets cause a doorbell to ring and a motor to turn. Imagine how different life would be without electric motors!

## Work On It

Magnets come in all shapes and sizes. The pictures to the right show many different types of magnets.

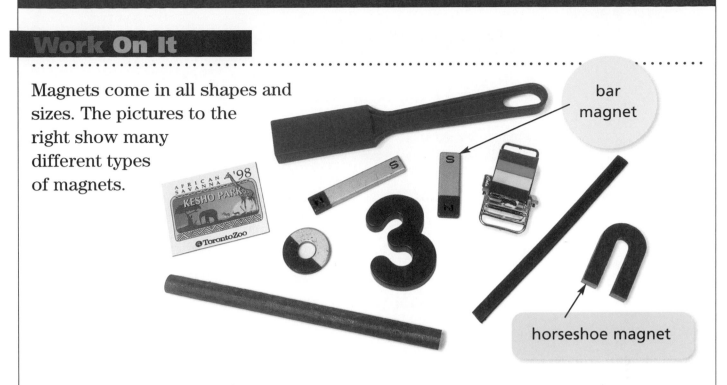

bar magnet

horseshoe magnet

**1.** Look at the pictures of different magnets.

**2.** Discuss with a partner where you have seen magnets like these.

Dropping a magnet or hitting it with something can make the magnet weaker or stop it from working. Magnets should not be heated. Keep magnets away from computers, videotapes, computer disks, and cassette tapes. They may not work if a magnet is kept near them.

## Communicate

You probably want to know more about what magnets can do. You must have a lot of questions about how they work.

**1.** Think of questions you have about magnets.

**2.** Draw three little bar magnets on a sheet of paper.

**3.** Draw three large bar magnets on a second sheet of paper.

**4.** Write your questions inside the pictures. Use the little pictures for little questions. Use the large pictures for really big questions that you might have to research.

# 2

# What Does a Magnet Pick Up?

Magnets pick up some objects and not others. When a magnet picks up an object, the object is called magnetic. The magnet picks it up. An object that is not picked up by a magnet is not magnetic. A magnet will not pick it up.

This magnet is holding paper on the refrigerator. The surface of the refrigerator is magnetic.

Soccer at 5:00

This magnet cannot pick up the paper because the paper is not magnetic.

The pictures above show one object that is magnetic and one object that is not magnetic. What other objects will a magnet pick up? You will find out in this investigation.

## What You Need ...........................................

- Objects to test with a magnet
- A magnet

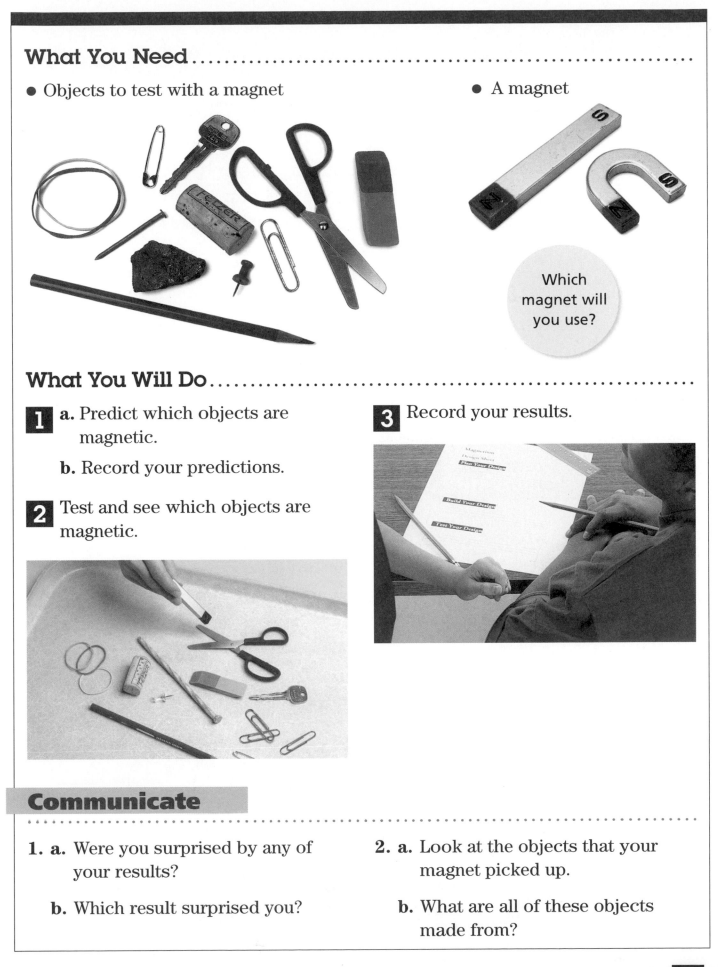

Which magnet will you use?

## What You Will Do ...........................................

**1** **a.** Predict which objects are magnetic.

**b.** Record your predictions.

**2** Test and see which objects are magnetic.

**3** Record your results.

## Communicate

**1. a.** Were you surprised by any of your results?

**b.** Which result surprised you?

**2. a.** Look at the objects that your magnet picked up.

**b.** What are all of these objects made from?

# 3  Does the Metal Matter?

You have learned that magnets only pick up metal objects. When a magnet picks up an object, we say that the magnet attracts the object. This attraction that a magnet has for some metals is called magnetism.

There are many types of metals.

Aluminum is used to make aluminum foil. Steel is used to make bridge beams. Copper is used to make pennies. Aluminum, steel, and copper are all metals.

## Work **On It**

Does a magnet attract all metal objects? Are some metals magnetic and some not magnetic? You will find out in this investigation.

## What You Need

- Metal objects to test with a magnet
- A magnet

## What You Will Do

 **1** Predict which metal objects the magnet will attract.

**2** Record your predictions.

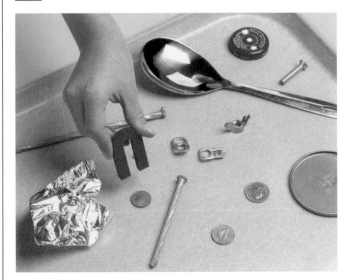

**3** Which metal objects are magnetic? Find out by testing them.

**4** Draw circles like the ones below in your notebook. Record your results in the circles.

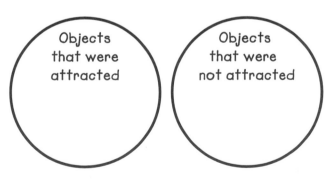

Objects that were attracted

Objects that were not attracted

## Communicate

. . . . . . . . . . . . . . . . . . . . . . . . . . . . . . . . . . . . . . . . . . . . . . . . . . . . . . . . . . .

**1.** What metals are the magnetic objects made from?

# Measuring Magnetic Strength

## Get Started

Some magnets are stronger than others. The size of the magnet does not always tell you how strong it is. Very small magnets can be strong. The strength of the magnet you use depends on what you need the magnet to do.

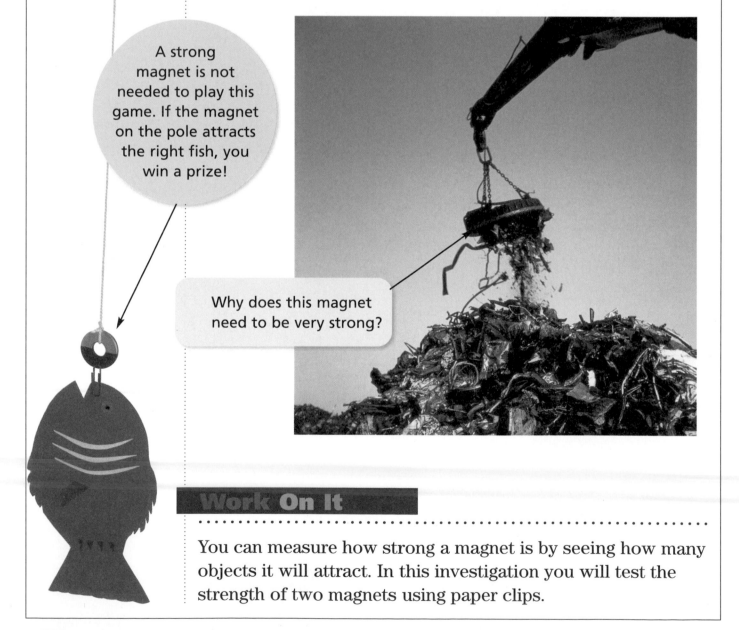

A strong magnet is not needed to play this game. If the magnet on the pole attracts the right fish, you win a prize!

Why does this magnet need to be very strong?

## Work On It

You can measure how strong a magnet is by seeing how many objects it will attract. In this investigation you will test the strength of two magnets using paper clips.

## What You Need

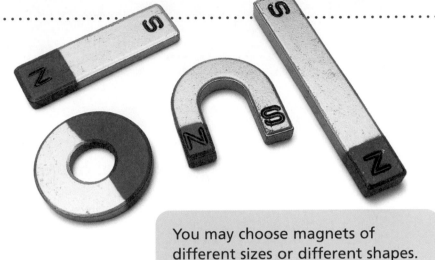

- Two different magnets
- A box of paper clips of the same size

> You may choose magnets of different sizes or different shapes.

## What You Will Do

**1** Predict which magnet is stronger and write down your prediction.

**2** Find out how many paper clips the first magnet can attract.

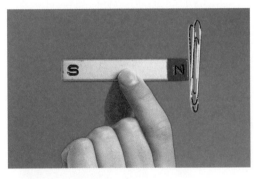

**3** Record this number.

**4** Find out how many paper clips the second magnet can attract and record this number.

## Communicate

**1. a.** Which of the two magnets you tested is stronger?

**b.** How do you know?

**2.** Compare your results with your classmates' results.

**a.** Who found the strongest magnet?

**b.** How many paper clips did it attract?

**Build** On What You Know

Try attracting paper clips with the middle of the magnet. Which part of a magnet is the strongest?

# 5

# What Makes It Magnetic?

You have learned that only certain types of metals are magnetic.

How are the magnetic metals you tested alike? They are all made of iron or nickel. Steel is made from iron, so objects made from steel are magnetic. A third metal called cobalt is also magnetic. The three magnetic metals are iron, nickel, and cobalt.

This tin can is made from iron. It has a coating of tin on it. Because there is iron in the can, it is magnetic.

This pop can is made from aluminum. It is not magnetic.

You have also learned that magnets can have different strengths. To make a magnet very strong, more than one type of metal is often used.

Marguerite will help you find more magnetic objects in her home. See what she finds in her garage.

Many parts of a car are magnetic. A magnet attracts the doors, the radio antenna, and the licence plate. What type of metal do you think these parts contain?

There are also magnetic parts on a bicycle. In this investigation you will find out where these parts are found.

## What You Need

- A strong magnet
- A bicycle

## What You Will Do

**1** Guess what parts of a bicycle are magnetic. Record your predictions.

**2** Use the magnet to see what parts of the bicycle it attracts.

**3** Record your results.

## Communicate

1. Make a list of five things on a bicycle that are not magnetic.

2. For each thing in your list in question 1, explain why it is not magnetic.

**Build** On What You Know

An automobile junkyard contains many car parts. How could a strong magnet be used to move some of these parts?

# Does Magnetism Pass Through Materials?

You know that light can pass through glass because you can see light shine on a table in front of a window. It is not as easy to tell if magnetism can pass through materials because magnetism is invisible.

This is made from a magnetic metal covered with plastic.

Magnetism is at work here, but it is invisible. The metal in the board can still attract a magnetic piece through the plastic.

You have already learned that cans made of iron are coated with tin. This is to help stop them from rusting. Tin-coated cans are magnetic. What other materials, besides tin, will magnetism pass through? Let's investigate and find out.

## What You Need

- A bar or wand magnet

This is a wand-shaped magnet.

- Materials to test

- A paper clip
- Some books

## What You Will Do

**1** Predict which materials magnetism will pass through and record your predictions.

**2** Set up your materials as shown in the photograph to the right.

**3** Carefully hold each material, one at a time, between the magnet and the paperclip.

**4** **a.** Does magnetism pass through the material?

**b.** Record your results.

## Communicate

**1.** What materials did magnetism pass through?

**2.** What materials did magnetism not pass through?

**Build** On What You Know

Think back to Activity 4. Guess what would happen if you tried to pick up plastic coated paper clips.

# Will Magnetism Pass Through Water?

## Get Started

In the last investigation you tested whether magnetism would pass through different materials. It would be a little tricky to test whether magnetism will pass through water in the same way!

> Scientists think some animals like whales can sense magnetism through water. This might explain how they find their way.

## Work On It

Plan an investigation that answers the question: Will magnetism pass through water? The way you set up your investigation must be different from the one you just did.

## What You Will Do ........................................

Follow the steps below to plan your investigation.

**Your Plan**

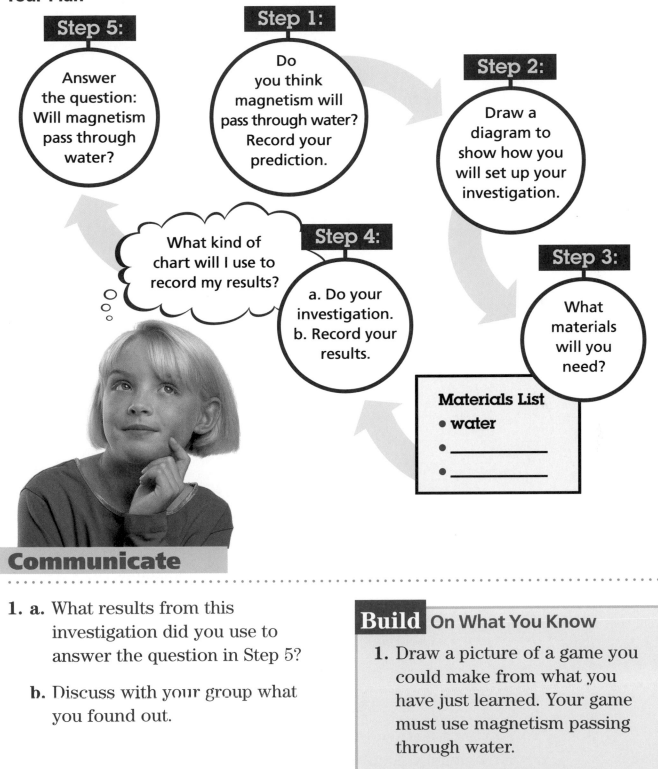

**Step 5:**
Answer the question: Will magnetism pass through water?

**Step 1:**
Do you think magnetism will pass through water? Record your prediction.

**Step 2:**
Draw a diagram to show how you will set up your investigation.

What kind of chart will I use to record my results?

**Step 4:**
a. Do your investigation.
b. Record your results.

**Step 3:**
What materials will you need?

**Materials List**
- water
- _____
- _____

## Communicate

1. **a.** What results from this investigation did you use to answer the question in Step 5?

   **b.** Discuss with your group what you found out.

**Build** On What You Know

1. Draw a picture of a game you could make from what you have just learned. Your game must use magnetism passing through water.

2. Give your game a title.

# Making Magnets

## Get Started

Do you wonder how the rock magnetite became a magnet? Scientists think that Earth may have made rocks like magnetite that contain iron into magnets. The core of Earth contains mostly iron and nickel. This makes Earth act like a giant magnet. Earth's magnetism may have turned the magnetite into a magnet over thousands of years. The rock was magnetized.

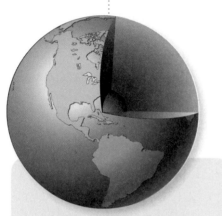

You can think of Earth as having a very large magnet in the centre of it.

Magnetized tools are very useful. How is a magnetized hammer useful? How is a screwdriver with a magnetized end useful?

## Work On It

You have learned that only the metals iron, nickel, and cobalt are magnetic. Could objects made of these metals be magnetized? Can they attract other metal objects? Can you magnetize another metal, such as copper? Let's find out.

## What You Need . . . . . . . . . . . . . . . . . . . . . . . . . . . . . . . . .

- An iron nail
- A nickel
- A penny

- A box of paper clips
- A magnet

## What You Will Do . . . . . . . . . . . . . . . . . . . . . . . . . . . . . . . .

**1** Stroke the nail with the magnet in one direction only. Drag the magnet down the nail. Then lift the magnet up and drag it down the nail again in the same direction.

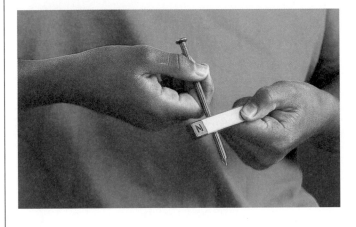

**2 a.** Test for magnetism after 10, 20, 30, and 40 strokes with the magnet.

**b.** Try to attract paper clips with the magnetized nail.

**3** Record your results in a chart.

**4 a.** Try to magnetize the nickel and the penny in the same way.

**b.** Record what happens.

## Communicate

1. Which objects became magnetized?

2. How do you know you made a magnet?

3. Would the nail be magnetized if it were stroked on the magnet instead of the way you did it?

4. Drop your new nail magnet on the floor.

   **a.** Is it still a magnet?

   **b.** How do you know?

### Build On What You Know

Think back to what you read about whales sensing magnetism through water. What big magnet could whales be sensing?

# The Poles of a Magnet

## Get Started

A magnet has two
ends called poles.

This end
is called the
south-seeking or
**south pole** of
the magnet.

This end
is called the
north-seeking or
**north pole** of
the magnet.

A compass on a ship or plane is used to find direction.
Remember that Earth is a magnet. The Earth attracts the needle
of a magnetic compass. A special compass is in the front of the
boat in the picture. It contains a floating magnet that is
attracted by the magnetism of Earth.

Earth and some compasses are magnets. Earth is a much larger magnet than a compass. Let's investigate what happens when two smaller magnets are near each other.

## What You Need

- Two bar magnets with the north and south poles marked on them

## What You Will Do

**1** Predict what will happen in each diagram below and record your predictions.

**2** Place the magnets as they are shown in the diagrams.

**3** Do not actually touch the magnets to each other. Just bring them close together.

**4** Record what happens.

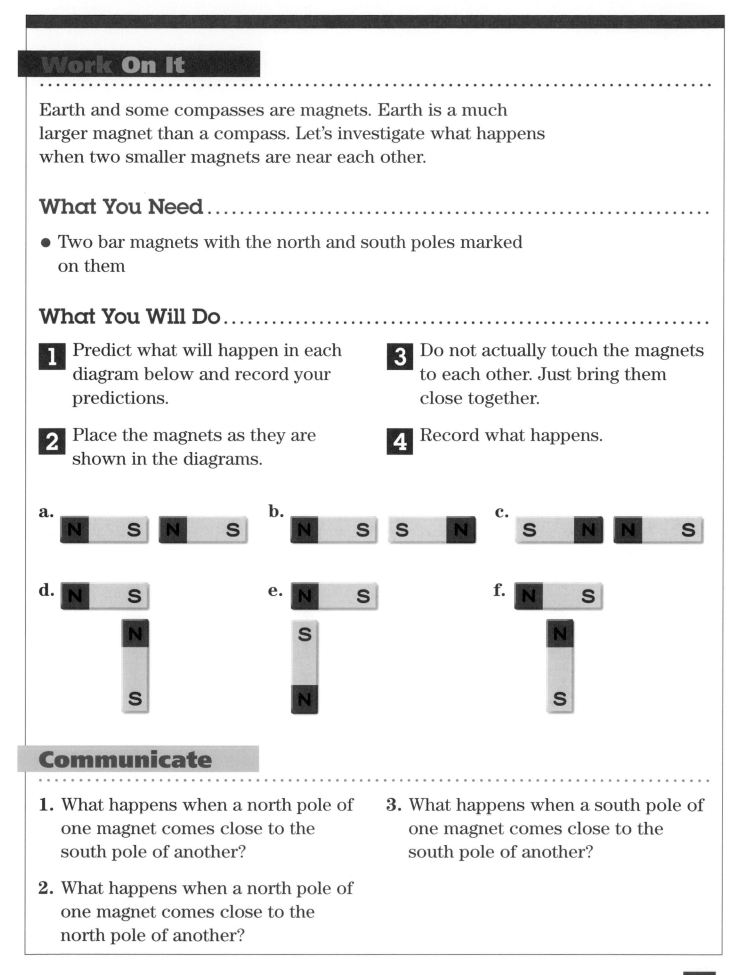

**a.** N S  N S

**b.** N S  S N

**c.** S N  N S

**d.** N S / N S

**e.** N S / S N

**f.** N S / N S

## Communicate

**1.** What happens when a north pole of one magnet comes close to the south pole of another?

**2.** What happens when a north pole of one magnet comes close to the north pole of another?

**3.** What happens when a south pole of one magnet comes close to the south pole of another?

# 10 Finding the North Pole

**Remember...**

**Unlike poles attract**

**Like poles repel**

You just found out what happens when the north pole of one magnet is brought close to the south pole of another magnet – the ends pull toward each other. They attract each other.

When the south pole of one magnet is brought close to the south pole of another magnet, the ends push apart. When two north poles are brought close to each other, the ends also push apart. They repel each other.

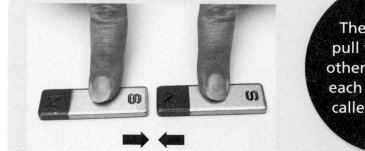

These magnets pull toward each other. They attract each other. This is called attraction.

These magnets push apart from each other. They repel each other. This is called repulsion.

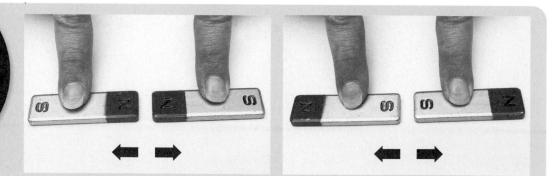

**Work On It**

This knowledge of attraction and repulsion is useful. It is how a compass works. You can use this knowledge to find the north pole of your homemade magnet.

## What You Need . . . . . . . . . . . . . . . . . . . . . . . . . . . . . . . . . . . . . . . . . . . . . .

- Your homemade magnet from **Activity 8: Making Magnets**
- A magnet with N and S poles marked on them

- Paper clips
- Heavy thread

## What You Will Do . . . . . . . . . . . . . . . . . . . . . . . . . . . . . . . . . . . . . . . . . . . .

**1** Test your homemade magnet to see that it is still magnetized.

**2** Hang the bar magnet from the edge of the desk using the thread.

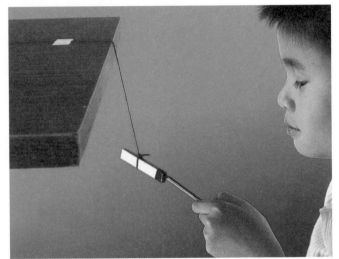

**3** Slowly bring one end of the nail to one pole of the bar magnet.

**4** Record what happens.

**5** Do the same with the other pole of the magnet and record your results.

## Communicate

1. How do you know which pole of your homemade magnet is north?

2. How do you know which pole of your homemade magnet is south?

3. Suppose you have a horseshoe magnet. Its poles are not labelled. How could you tell which pole is north?

# 11 Charged Materials

OUCH!

Has this happened to you? You walk across a carpet in a pair of socks, touch a doorknob, and zap! You get a shock.

Scientists believe everything is made up of tiny particles. They are too small to see with your eyes or even a microscope. Rubbing some materials can cause some of these particles to move. Walking across a carpet can cause your socks to pick up some particles from the carpet. Your socks, and even your body, now have extra particles. They are charged.

When you touch a doorknob, the extra particles jump from you to the doorknob. Just like magnetism, the jumping of these particles is invisible. You can't see it, but you sure can feel it! Sometimes you can also hear it.

What you are feeling is static electricity.

Static electricity occurs when charges build up in one place. It is different from the other kind of electricity in the wires of your home. You will investigate static electricity in this activity.

## What You Need

- 2 balloons tied separately with 0.5 m light string
- Piece of wool fabric
- Piece of nylon fabric

## What You Will Do

You will charge the balloons three times:

- First, rub them with wool fabric.
- Next, rub them with nylon fabric.
- The third time, rub one balloon with wool and the other one with nylon.

Follow these steps each time you charge the balloons.

**1 Predict**
   a. Guess what will happen before you charge the balloons.
   b. Use the words **attract** and **repel** in your predictions.

**2 Charge**
To charge a balloon rub it quickly back and forth on the fabric.

**3 Find Out**
Hold the balloons by the strings after they are charged. Slowly bring them close together.

**4 Record**
Record what happens after each test.

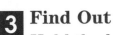

## Communicate

1. How did the charged balloons act like the magnets in **Activity 9: The Poles of a Magnet?**

2. a. Did the wool and the nylon materials give the balloons the same charge?
   b. How do you know?

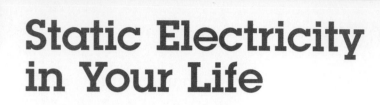

# Static Electricity in Your Life

## Get Started

Do you remember when you last got a shock after walking across a carpet in your socks? What season of the year was it?

Static electricity most often occurs when the air is cool and dry. That is why you feel more static electricity in winter. Charges can build up in winter because the air contains less moisture than in summer. It is less humid. Many people add moisture to the air in their homes in winter.

Charged particles can also build up in your hair when you comb it.

Charges build up in a clothes dryer. Sometimes fabric softener is added to the laundry. It stops static electricity from forming.

Sometimes static electricity can be dangerous.

1. Look at the following picture. A fuel truck is putting gasoline into tanks at a station.

2. Discuss with a partner why a spark from static electricity is dangerous here.

## Communicate

1. How can you get static electricity out of your hair?

2. Why do charges build up in dry air and not humid air?

### Build On What You Know

Think back to what you did in the activity **Charged Materials**. How can you make a charged balloon lose its charge?

# Lightning: Nature's Static Electricity

## Get Started

Lightning is static electricity in nature. Charged particles build up in the clouds. When there are too many charged particles they can jump to a nearby cloud. You see this jump as lightning.

Charged particles from clouds can also jump to a tree or building. They jump to the tallest object.

Static electricity can travel through some materials and not others. A material that will allow static electricity to travel through it is called a conductor. Metals are conductors. Water is also a conductor. A material that does not allow static electricity to travel through it is called an insulator. Rubber is an insulator.

This building has a lightning rod. It is a long, pointed metal rod attached to a wire that goes to the ground. A lightning rod is a conductor that carries the static electricity to the ground and stops the lightning from setting the building on fire.

## Work On It

What can you do to stay safe in a thunderstorm?
Here are some safety rules to follow:

1. If you are indoors, stay away from windows, doors, bathtubs, sinks, electrical appliances, and telephones.
2. If you are outside, don't take shelter under a tree.
3. Stay inside a vehicle.
4. If you are in the open, stay low to the ground. Squat or kneel instead of lying down.
5. If you are on a hill or high point of ground, go to the valley or gully.
6. If you are swimming or boating, go to the shore.

Discuss with your classmates what each of these rules tells you about conductors and insulators.

## Communicate

1. Why should you get out of the water during a lightning storm?
2. Name one material that is a good conductor.
3. If you are inside a car, what part of the car would insulate you from lightning?
4. Name one material that is a good insulator.

# How Important Is Distance?

## Get Started

Metal detectors use magnetism. A light on the handle turns on when a metal object is found.

Some people use metal detectors to search for buried objects. Metal detectors are also used in airports. People walk through them before they get on an airplane. They are used so dangerous weapons cannot be taken on airplanes.

## Work On It

A metal object has to be close enough for the metal detector to sense it. As the distance between the metal object and the metal detector gets larger, the attraction gets smaller.

Distance affects static electric charges the same way. They get weaker as the objects get farther apart. In this activity, you will look at the difference distance makes.

## What You Need................................

- A charged balloon
- A metre stick
- A paper clip on a thread
- A ping pong ball
- A bar magnet

## What You Will Do................................

**1** Set up your investigation as shown in the photographs below. Do one part of the investigation at a time.

**2** **a.** Predict how close the charged balloon must be to get the ping pong ball to move.

**b.** Write down your prediction.

**3** Slowly bring the charged balloon closer to the ping pong ball until the ball moves.

**4** Measure this distance and record your result.

**5** Repeat these steps with the magnet and the paper clip to see how distance affects magnetism.

## Communicate

1. What happens to static electric attraction as the distance between the objects gets smaller?

2. What happens to magnetic attraction as the distance between the objects gets larger?

3. How did your results compare to your predictions?

**Build** **On What You Know**

What will happen if a compass is very close to a magnet?

# Magnetic Boats and Sleds

## Get Started

Some trains are designed to use magnetic force. There is a magnet underneath the train in the picture, and the train track is magnetic. The train and track are designed so they repel each other. This lifts the train up.

## Work On It

### Design It

Now you will use what you have learned about magnetism. You will design and build your own vehicle that moves using magnetism. Recording your ideas on a design sheet will help you plan.

1. Choose one of the vehicle choices below.

2. Look to see what your boat or sled has to do.

3. Record your choice and what your vehicle must do.

| Design Choice #1 | Design Choice #2 |
| --- | --- |
| Design and build a boat that moves using magnetism. | Design and build a sled that moves using magnetism. |
| Your boat must be able to: | Your sled must be able to: |
| • Move around a tub of water<br>• Hold ten marbles and still float | • Move up and down a paper hill<br>• Hold a small toy person |

## Plan Your Design

**1.** Brainstorm many designs for your vehicle.

**2.** How will you decide which is the best design?

**3.** Record your ideas.

Here are some of the things you might use to build your vehicle. What other things could you use?

## Build Your Design

1. What problems did you have during the building?

2. What did you do to solve them?

3. Record your problems and solutions.

## Test Your Design

1. Check to see that your boat or sled does what it is supposed to do. Does your boat float? Does your sled move up and down the paper hill?

2. Do you need to make changes to your design after you have tested it?

3. Record whether your design was successful.

## Communicate

1. Show the rest of the class how your boat or sled moves by magnetic force.

# How Well Did You Do?

Now it is time to see how well you did with your design project. Use this chart to help you score your work. Four stars is the highest score.

| 1 Star | 2 Stars | 3 Stars | 4 Stars |
|---|---|---|---|

## SAFETY

**1. a. How well did you follow safety rules when building your vehicle?**

| ⭐ | ⭐⭐ | ⭐⭐⭐ | ⭐⭐⭐⭐ |
|---|---|---|---|
| You had to be reminded to follow the safety rules. | You followed some of the safety rules. | You followed most of the safety rules. | You followed all of the safety rules. |

**b. How safely did you use equipment like scissors and glue?**

| ⭐ | ⭐⭐ | ⭐⭐⭐ | ⭐⭐⭐⭐ |
|---|---|---|---|
| You had to be reminded to use equipment and materials safely. | You used equipment and materials safely some of the time. | You used equipment and materials safely most of the time. | You used equipment and materials safely. |

## FINISHED VEHICLE

**2. How well does your finished vehicle (boat or sled) do what it is supposed to do?**

| ⭐ | ⭐⭐ | ⭐⭐⭐ | ⭐⭐⭐⭐ |
|---|---|---|---|
| It does none of the things it is supposed to do. | It does one thing it is supposed to do. | It does both of the things it is supposed to do some of the time. | It does both of the things it is supposed to do all the time. |

## RECORDING YOUR DESIGN

### 3. a. Planning

⭐ You had one idea about your vehicle when you first planned it.

⭐⭐ You had two ideas about your vehicle when you first planned it.

⭐⭐⭐ You had three ideas about your vehicle when you first planned it.

⭐⭐⭐⭐ You had four ideas about your vehicle when you first planned it.

### b. Building

⭐ You did not describe challenges you had in building or how you solved them.

⭐⭐ You described a challenge that you had in building but not what you did to solve it.

⭐⭐⭐ You described one challenge you had during building and what you did to solve it.

⭐⭐⭐⭐ You described two challenges you had during building and what you did to solve them.

### c. Testing

⭐ You did not record how you tested your vehicle or you did not test it.

⭐⭐ How you tested your vehicle is not well described.

⭐⭐⭐ You described how you tested your vehicle to see that it did what it was supposed to do.

⭐⭐⭐⭐ You described how you tested your vehicle to see that it did what it was supposed to do. You also described changes that you made.

## Demonstrate What You Know

### Get Started

Marguerite took some photos while you were learning about magnetic and charged particles. Here are some photos from her album.

## Work On It

1. Look at the photos from Marguerite's album.

2. Record a sentence about each photo. The sentence should say something about what you have learned.

3. Write each sentence on a blank card. You are making a deck of facts.

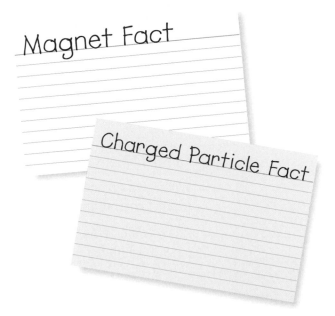

4. Now, make two cards that tell how magnets are used in the world. Make two cards about examples of charged particles in the world.

## Communicate

How well did you do at making your fact cards? Use this information to score your work. Four stars is the highest score for each part.

## Part 1

Give yourself four stars if you have written three facts about magnetism and three facts about charged particles.

## Part 2

Give yourself four stars if you have correctly used six new words in your facts.

## Part 3

Give yourself four stars if you have:

● written two facts about the use of magnets in the world

● written two facts on examples of charged particles in the world

# Review

## Explain Your Stuff

### What did you learn about magnetic and charged materials?

1. Use the letters below to make a list of objects that magnets will not attract.

   W _____    R _____

   V _____    S _____

   E _____    C _____

   P _____    G _____

2. Each bar magnet below contains a letter. Using each letter, record the name of an object that is magnetic.

3. Name three ways magnets are used in each place below:

   **a.** your school

   **b.** your home

4. Name three shapes of magnets.

5. What could you put on a pencil so it is attracted to a magnet?

6. How can you make a magnet stop working or not work very well?

7. Match up the words from Column A with a definition in Column B.

| Column A | Column B |
|---|---|
| pole | Moisture in the air |
| static electricity | This is a natural magnet |
| attraction | Will not allow static electricity to pass through |
| insulator | |
| magnetite | When 2 objects push apart from each other |
| conductor | |
| humid | Charges built up in one place |
| repulsion | The attraction that a magnet has for some metals |
| magnetism | |
| | The end of a magnet |
| | When two objects pull toward each other |
| | Allows static electricity to pass through it |

8. Name two ways Marguerite could get rid of her problem with static electricity.

## How Did You Do?

1. List one thing you didn't know about magnets before this unit started.

2. List one thing you didn't know about charged materials before this unit started.

3. Give one reason why what you learned about magnetism and charged materials is important.

4. What work are you most proud of in this unit?

## Now you know a lot about magnetic and charged materials. Here are some of the things you've learned:

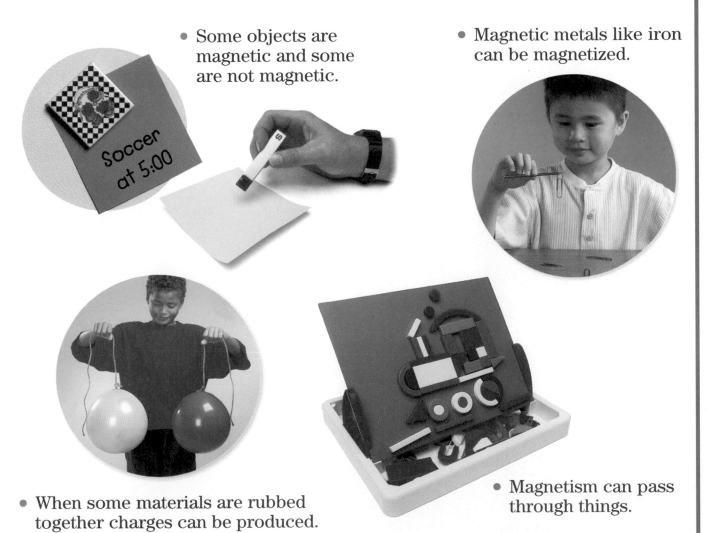

- Some objects are magnetic and some are not magnetic.

- Magnetic metals like iron can be magnetized.

- When some materials are rubbed together charges can be produced.

- Magnetism can pass through things.

Soccer at 5:00

- Static electricity can be avoided.

- Magnetic and static attraction get weaker when the distance gets larger.

- There are many examples of magnetic and charged materials in your life.

# Glossary

**attract** to pull toward each other

**charged** the extra particles on an object that cause static electricity

**conductor** lets static electricity travel through it

**insulator** stops static electricity from travelling through it

**magnetic** can be picked up by a magnet

**magnetism** the attraction a magnet has for an object

**magnetize** to make an object a magnet

**poles** the opposite ends of a magnet

**repel** to push apart

**static electricity** a buildup of charged particles

# Acknowledgments

The publisher wishes to thank the following sources for photographs, illustrations, articles, and other materials used in this book. Care has been taken to determine and locate ownership of copyrighted material used in this text. We will gladly receive information enabling us to rectify any errors or omissions in credits.

## Photography

p. 1 Jim Allor Photography,  p. 4 Albert J. Copley/Visuals Unlimited, p. 5 Dave Starrett, p. 6 Dave Starrett, p. 7 (top) Dave Starrett, p. 7 (bottom) Ray Boudreau, p. 8 (left) Alan Sirulnikoff/First Light, p. 8 (right) Dave Starrett , p. 9 (top) Dave Starrett, p. 9 (bottom) Ray Boudreau, p. 10 (left) Dave Starrett, p. 10 (right) Alex Bartel/Science Photo Library/Publiphoto, p. 11 (top) Dave Starrett, p. 11 (bottom) Ray Boudreau, p. 12 Dave Starrett, p. 14 Dave Starrett, p. 15 (top) Dave Starrett, p. 15 (bottom) Ray Boudreau, p. 16 Thomas Kitchin/First Light, p. 17 Ray Boudreau, p. 18 (right & bottom) Dave Starrett, p. 19 Ray Boudreau, p. 20 Dave Starrett, p. 22 Dave Starrett, p. 23 Ray Boudreau, p. 25 Ray Boudreau, p. 26 Ray Boudreau, p. 27 Kennon Cooke/Valan Photos, p. 28 CP Picture Archives (Adrian Wyld), p. 29 Deneve Feigh Bunde/Visuals Unlimited, p. 31 Ray Boudreau, pp. 32–33 Michael S. Yamashita/Corbis, p. 34 (top) Ray Boudreau, p. 34 (bottom) Dave Starrett, p. 35 Ray Boudreau, p. 38 Ray Boudreau, p. 41 (top left & centre, bottom right) Dave Starrett, p. 41 (top right, bottom left) Ray Boudreau, p. 42 (left) Deneve Feigh Bunde/Visuals Unlimited, p. 42 (right & centre) Ray Boudreau

## Illustration

Albert Molnar: p. 1, pp. 2–3, p. 13, p. 20, p. 24, p. 30, p. 40, p. 42
Jun Park: p. 18 (left)

## Cover Photograph

PhotoDisc, Inc.